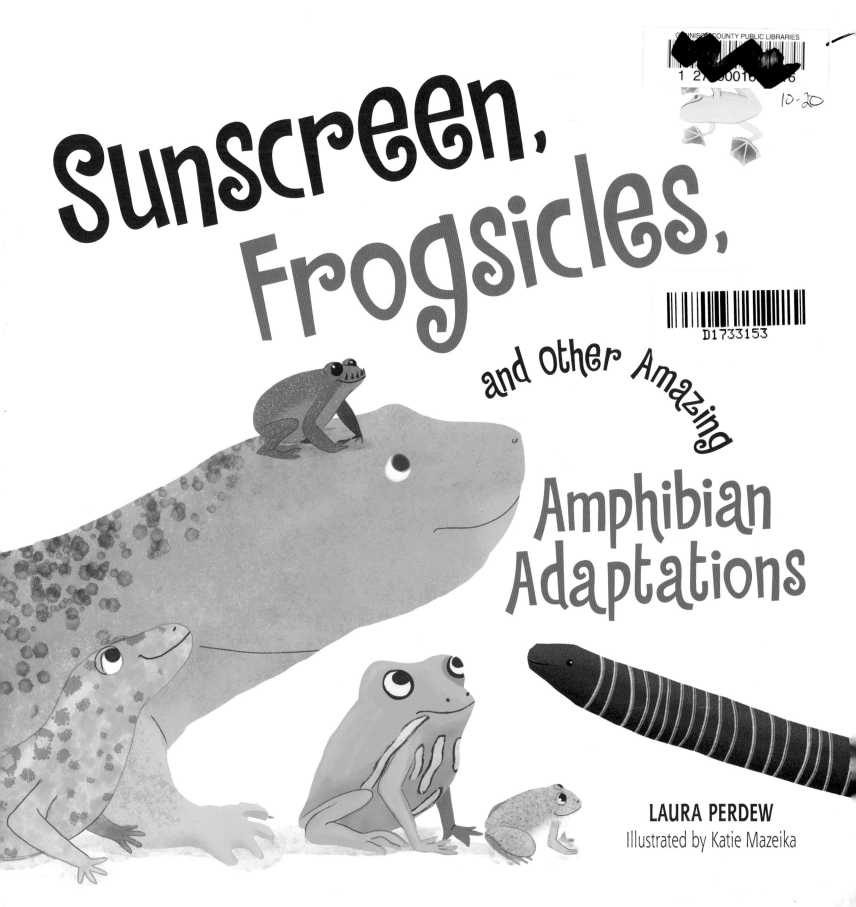

Sunscreen, Frogsicles, and Other Amazing Amphibian Adaptations

LAURA PERDEW

Illustrated by Katie Mazeika

Amphibian Cinquain

Emei Moustache Toad

Amphibian
Barbed, ready
Fighting, wrestling, stabbing,
Uses his cool barbed moustache
Toad

Wallace's Flying Frog

Amphibian
Emerald, acrobatic
Leaping, gliding, landing
Escapes danger by flying
Frog

Alaskan Wood Frog

Amphibian
Tough, camouflaged
Freezing, thawing, hopping
Frogsicle in the winter
Wood frog

Amphibians have many amazing adaptations to help them survive.

Have you heard of the strange-looking axolotl? It can regrow body parts. Maybe you already know about the tiny poison dart frogs in South America that are DEADLY poisonous.

But do you know how waxy monkey tree frogs protect their skin from the sun?

Sunscreen!

Just like people, waxy monkey tree frogs put on sunscreen.

These large frogs are found in the treetops of dry forests in South America.

But they're not protecting themselves from sunburn. They use the sunscreen to keep their skin from drying out. Their bodies produce a waxy substance that they rub all over their skin.

With their super-flexible arms and legs, they can reach tricky places all over their bodies!

3

While waxy monkey tree frogs need to protect themselves from the hot sun, Alaskan wood frogs need protection from the cold winter.

In the winter, wood frogs freeze solid. Even their hearts stop beating!

They become frogsicles!

When the temperature drops, wood frogs freeze over and wait until spring. Then, as the air warms, they thaw out and hop away. How?

They have natural antifreeze in their blood.

Water-holding frogs have to survive a different kind of weather—the dry spells in Australia. To do this, they burrow deep underground while the soil is still soggy.

Then, they shed their skins and use them to create cocoons.

It's like a sleeping bag made of skin.

Water-holding frogs can stay buried for up to two years!

When the rain returns, they break out of the cocoons and hop along on their merry way.

Sirens create cocoons, too, if they need to wait out a dry period. But instead of using skin, sirens make cocoons out of mucus.

Mucus is a fancy word for a snot-like slime.

Ick?

Not for these two-legged salamanders that love mud and shallow water! Those snot cocoons help them survive until their habitat fills with water again.

Sirens are a
type of
salamander.

It has a beak,
only two
front legs,
and gills.

Hellbender salamanders are always covered
in a slimy layer of mucus.

This gives them a very unique nickname—snot otter!

Hellbenders live their whole lives in water, but they don't have gills.

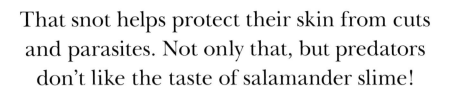

That snot helps protect their skin from cuts
and parasites. Not only that, but predators
don't like the taste of salamander slime!

Would you want your dinner covered in slime?

They breathe through their skin.

Hellbenders might taste icky, but some types of caecilians have skin that's yummy enough for the babies to eat!

Yup, some mother caecilians grow a special layer of skin after giving birth. And their young have short, rounded teeth that are perfect for peeling off that skin for a meal!

Gross?

Not for a baby caecilian. That skin contains
the fat and nutrients they need to grow.

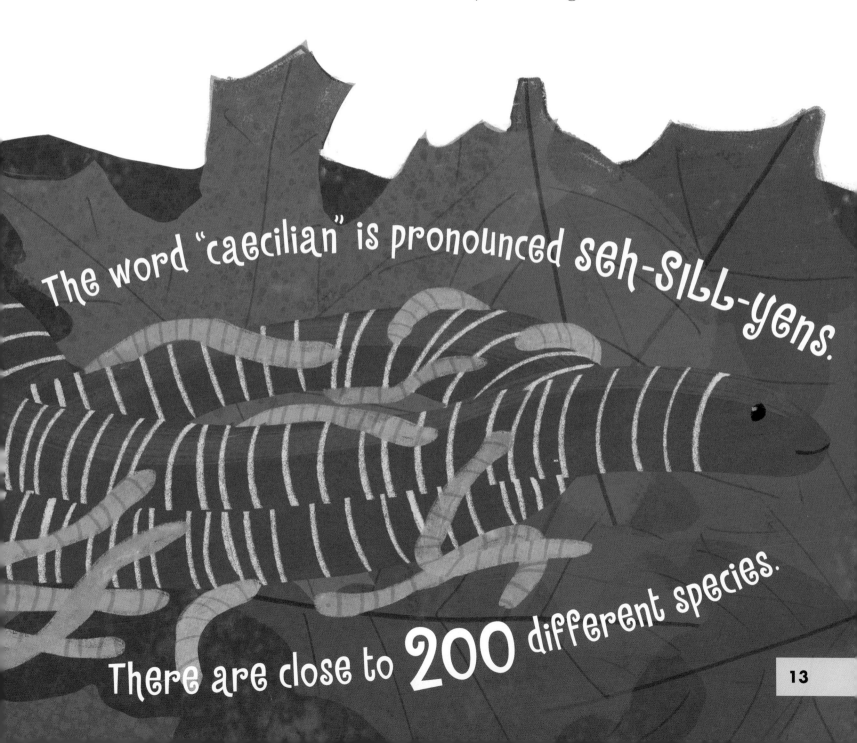

The word "caecilian" is pronounced seh-SILL-yens.

There are close to 200 different species.

Surinam toad moms use the skin on their
backs for their babies in a very different way.

That's where they carry their eggs!

The female's skin grows over every egg,
so each one has its own cozy pocket.

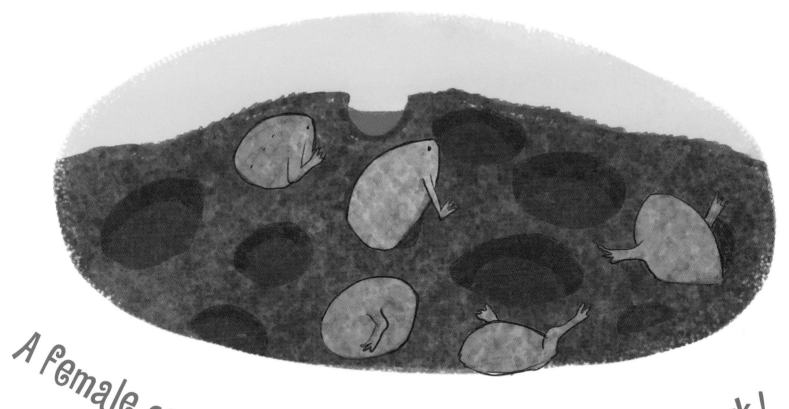

A female can carry up to **100** eggs on her back!

Even after hatching, the toadlets stay on their mom's back under the skin. When they are fully formed, toadlet arms, legs, and snouts push out of the pockets.

Off they go!

The punk rocker frog has amazing skin, too—but it's not for babies. It's for safety.

These tiny frogs are shapeshifters!

This frog was just discovered in 2009.

Scientists are still learning about it.

Their skin can go from smooth to spiky in a matter of minutes! Scientists have observed that these spikes are used as camouflage, not weapons.

Wouldn't it be fun to be able to shapeshift to fit your environment?

Spanish ribbed newts
are a different kind of
shape-shifter. When attacked,
they defend themselves by
using their own ribs as weapons.

Just think!
If you were a Spanish ribbed newt,
you could push your ribs
out through your skin
and ta-da!

**You could defend yourself
with your poisonous barbs!**

Pushing its ribs through its skin does not harm the newt. The torn tissue regrows quickly.

What is a critter to do if it can't use its ribs in a fight?
Male Emei moustache toads use their moustaches!

Seriously? Yes!

But they aren't hairy moustaches—these
are made of spikes. During mating season,
males grow these moustaches to defend
their nesting sites from other males.

And if one spike falls off?
No problem. A new one will grow in its place.

The 10 to 16 moustache spikes that grow on males are made of keratin . . .

. . . just like your fingernails and hair!

Many amphibians have poison or spikes to defend themselves or use in a fight. But certain frogs in Madagascar have size on their side.

They are very tiny!

Scientists recently discovered these miniature frogs and named them

Mini mum,
Mini scule, and
Mini ature.

Can you guess how being small helps?
These frogs hunt mini prey and can easily hide so they don't become prey themselves!

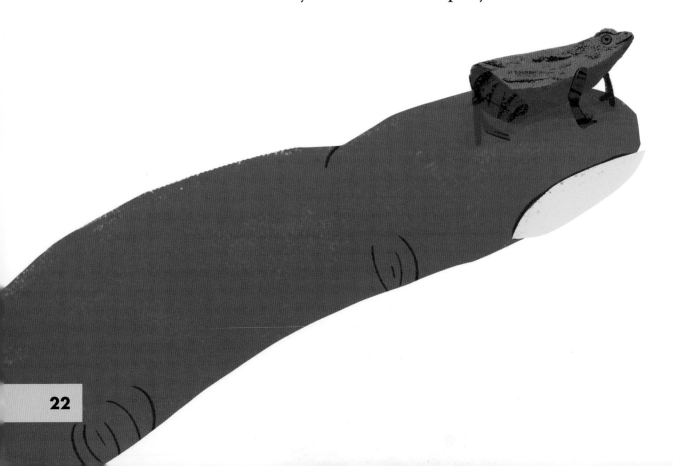

The smallest of these frogs is only a little longer than a grain of rice!

Wallace's flying frogs aren't very big either.

To avoid danger, these frogs use their enormous webbed feet.

But not to swim away.

To fly!

Well, glide.

Wallace's flying frogs spend their lives in the trees.

They use those feet as parachutes. This unusual adaptation helps the frogs move easily from tree to tree through the jungle. Not only that, they have special sticky footpads to help them stick wherever they land.

They come to the ground only to mate and lay eggs.

How do baby amphibians stay safe?
If you are a Darwin's frog, you go to daddy daycare!

Darwin's frog dads keep their tadpoles in
sacs in their throats. The tadpoles even
go through metamorphosis there.

Once the frogs are fully formed,
they emerge. When they do, it looks like the dads are

barfing up froglets!

Every amphibian has its own
amazing adaptations!

What are some others you can find?

Scientists have observed as many as **19 BABIES** in a frog dad's sac.

27

Amphibians Near You

Amphibians are found all around the world, except Antarctica. That means there are amphibians living near you! And every amphibian has many adaptations that help it survive. They must be able to find food, take shelter, and stay safe.

Emei moustache toad

credit: Cameron M. Hudson, Jinzhong Fu (CC BY 2.5)

WHAT YOU NEED

a notebook and paper, research materials

WHAT YOU DO

Choose an amphibian to study that lives near you. Find out what adaptations it has. Some of these adaptations have to do with how the amphibian looks. Other adaptations have to do with how it acts.

You might go to a zoo or aquarium to talk to an expert. You can visit a park and talk to a ranger.

Head to the library and find books and websites for more information. How many adaptations can you identify?

Now, draw or find a picture of your amphibian. Then, share your research on all of the amphibian's adaptations with your friends!

Axolotl

Glossary

adaptation: something about a plant or animal that helps it survive in its habitat.

amphibian: a cold-blooded animal, such as a toad, frog or salamander, that needs sunlight to keep warm and shade to stay cool. Amphibians live on land and in the water.

antifreeze: a substance that keeps something from freezing.

camouflage: colors or patterns that allow a plant or animal to blend in with its environment.

cinquain: a short poem that usually has 22 syllables within five lines.

cocoon: a protective covering.

cold-blooded: describes animals that need sunlight to keep warm and shade to stay cool, such as toads, frogs or salamanders.

environment: the area in which something lives.

gills: an animal part that lets the creature get oxygen out of the water to breathe.

habitat: an area that a plant or animal calls home.

keratin: a substance that forms fingernails, beaks, hair, feathers, and claws.

mating: reproducing to make something new, just like itself. To make babies.

metamorphosis: an animal's complete change in physical form as it develops into an adult.

mucus: a slippery substance produced in bodies and used for protection.

nutrients: substances that living things need to live and grow.

parasite: a living thing that feeds off another living thing.

predator: an animal that hunts another animal for food.

prey: an animal that is hunted and eaten by another animal.

species: a group of living things that are closely related and produce young.

substance: the material that something is made of.

CHECK OUT THE OTHER TITLES IN THIS SET!

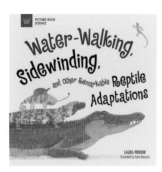

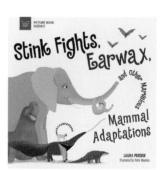

Nomad Press

A division of Nomad Communications

10 9 8 7 6 5 4 3 2 1

This book was manufactured by CGB Printers, North Mankato, Minnesota, United States
August 2020, Job #300936
ISBN Softcover: 978-1-61930-964-7
ISBN Hardcover: 978-1-61930-961-6

Educational Consultant, Marla Conn

Questions regarding the ordering of this book should be addressed to
Nomad Press
2456 Christian St., White River Junction, VT 05001
www.nomadpress.net

Printed in the United States.